THOMAS KINKADE
Studios
PAINT with WATER
Through the Seasons

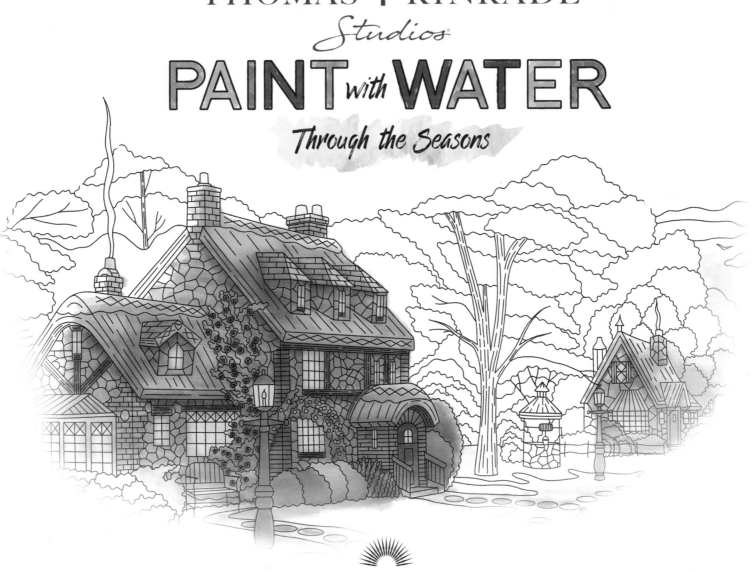

THUNDER BAY
P · R · E · S · S

San Diego, California

Thunder Bay Press
An imprint of Printers Row Publishing Group
9717 Pacific Heights Blvd., San Diego, CA 92121
www.thunderbaybooks.com • mail@thunderbaybooks.com

THOMAS KINKADE
Studios

Copyright © 2024 Thomas Kinkade Studios.
Images © 1997–2021 Thomas Kinkade Studios.

Printers Row Publishing Group is a division of Readerlink Distribution Services, LLC.
Thunder Bay Press is a registered trademark of Readerlink Distribution Services, LLC.

Correspondence regarding the content of this book should be sent to Thunder Bay Press, Editorial Department, at the above address.

Thunder Bay Press
Publisher: Peter Norton
Associate Publisher: Ana Parker
Art Director: Charles McStravick
Senior Developmental Editor: Diane Cain
Editor: Sara Maher
Production Team: Beno Chan, Mimi Oey
Designer: Erica Skatzes
Illustrator: Erica Skatzes

ISBN: 978-1-6672-0545-8

Printed, manufactured, and assembled in Rawang, Selangor, Malaysia.
First printing October 2023. THP/10/23

27 26 25 24 23   1 2 3 4 5

PAINT A BEAUTIFUL WORLD

From blooming gardens and idyllic cottages to soaring mountains and crashing seas, the paintings of Thomas Kinkade are instantly recognizable. Beyond Thom's signature painting style of luminism, which focuses on clarity of light, the images evoke feelings of comfort, tranquility, and peace.

This collection of 36 of Thom's most-loved paintings shows the world moving through nature's magnificent seasons. As you paint, find gratitude and serenity in the precious new life and hope of spring; the radiant glow and romance of summer; the transforming landscape and bountiful harvest of autumn; and the simple pleasures and cozy traditions of winter.

ABOUT THOMAS KINKADE

In the very beginning of his artistic career, Thomas Kinkade put his entire life savings into the printing of his first lithograph. Inspired not by fame and fortune, Thom found his purpose in the simple act of painting straight from the heart, putting on canvas the natural wonders and images that moved him most.

Though the recipient of countless awards and honors, it was Thom's profound sense of purpose that his art was not just an accessory, but also a ministry, that

continues as his legacy. Over the years he shared his joy and used his paints in support of hospitals, schools, and humanitarian relief. Thom's dearest wish had always been that his artwork would be a messenger of hope and inspiration to others—a message to slow down, appreciate the little details in life, and to look for beauty in the world around us. As millions of collectors around the world sit back and enjoy his artwork in their homes, there is no doubt that Thomas Kinkade had indeed achieved his goal of Sharing the Light™.

PAINT WITH LIGHT . . . AND WATER!

Experience nature's many wonders as the picturesque world
of Thomas Kinkade transitions from season to season.

1. Use the Paintings Key
   on the inside back cover
   and flap to choose your
   next project. Check the
   page number, which is
   listed next to the name
   of the painting.

2. Turn to the correct
   page in the book. To
   preserve the beauty
   of your painting, the
   page number is located
   to the left of the page
   perforation, close to
   the spine.

3. Slip the back cover flap underneath your painting page to prevent water from seeping onto another page.

4. Dip the included paintbrush into clean water. Give the brush a gentle tap to remove any excess water.

5. Glide your paintbrush over the black lines to reveal vibrant colors.

Thomas Kinkade
STUDIOS

Thomas
Kinkade
STUDIOS

Thomas Kinkade
STUDIOS

Miss Merritt

Thomas
Kinkade
STUDIOS

Thomas Kinkade STUDIOS

Thomas Kinkade
STUDIOS

Thomas Kinkade
STUDIOS

MICHELANGELO'S

Cafe

Thomas
Kinkade
STUDIOS

5

Thomas Kinkade
STUDIOS

Thomas Kinkade
STUDIOS

Thomas
Kinkade
STUDIOS

73

Thomas Kinkade STUDIOS

Thomas Kinkade STUDIOS